Original title:
Island Vibes

Copyright © 2025 Creative Arts Management OÜ
All rights reserved.

Author: Isaac Ravenscroft
ISBN HARDBACK: 978-1-80581-518-1
ISBN PAPERBACK: 978-1-80581-045-2
ISBN EBOOK: 978-1-80581-518-1

Misty Mornings and Moonlit Nights

Mornings tease with fog so thick,
Coffee spills, it's quite the trick.
Seagulls dance, they squawk with glee,
While I dodge the waves - oh me!

Moonlit nights bring laughter loud,
Crabs join in; they're quite the crowd.
With a splash, my friends all yell,
As they slip and trip - oh, what the hell!

Sunsets like Silk

Evening skies of orange and pink,
We race for the beach, don't stop to think.
With flip-flops flying through the air,
In the sand, we lose our flair.

The sun dips down, a perfect sight,
But we're here for snacks - that's our delight.
A seagull swoops, nabbing our fries,
We shriek and laugh as it quickly flies!

Barefoot Adventures

Barefoot on the sandy shore,
I scream as I step on something sore.
Was it a shell or just my luck?
I hop around - I'm such a cluck!

Chasing crabs, oh what a chase,
They scuttle fast, it's quite a race.
Fallen coconuts roll like balls,
I dodge and weave, against the walls!

Nature's Gentle Embrace

Gentle waves tickle my toes,
While I trip over seaweed grows.
"Oh look, a starfish!" I loudly shout,
But it rolls away, so what's that about?

Palm trees sway in the balmy breeze,
I misjudge the height and bump my knees.
Nature laughs with every silly move,
In this paradise, we find our groove!

Horizon of Happiness

Laughing gulls dance on the breeze,
Sunscreen fights the tan with ease.
Flip-flops chatter on the shore,
While sandcastles start to snore.

A crab scuttles, doing the jig,
As children giggle at his big wig.
Seagulls steal chips with delight,
Sun-kissed days stretch into night.

Twilight by the Sea

Mango drinks spill on the sand,
A dog with shades plays in the band.
The sunset's colors start to blend,
And beach balls bounce without an end.

Laughter echoes, waves in play,
A dolphin's flip steals the show today.
Sandy toes and giggles abound,
As twilight wraps the world around.

Driftwood Reverie

A piece of driftwood claims its throne,
Wearing shells like a king's own stone.
Octopus friend joins the odd parade,
As fish gossip, unafraid.

Beachcombers treasure their finds,
A flip-flop's wanderer, one of a kind.
They chase the tide, then must flee,
For seaweed hugs them like a tree.

Sealed with a Seashell

Messages sealed in a seashell tight,
Whispers of waves in the pale moonlight.
Tide pools giggling at the jokes,
A sea star winks at nearby folks.

Kites flying high with silly grace,
The ocean grins, a merry face.
Laughter bubbles in the salty air,
As flip-flops race, a comical affair.

Gentle Swells

The waves are giggling, what a sound,
They tickle toes, both lost and found.
A crab in a hat dances on the sand,
While seagulls argue, oh, isn't it grand?

The sun wears shades, looking quite cool,
A fish with a grin jumps, breaking the rule.
Surfboards are laughing, catching the breeze,
As turtles do yoga, oh, such a tease!

Embrace of the Tropical Sun

In flip-flops we shuffle with drinks in hand,
A parrot is gossiping, isn't it grand?
Sandy toes wiggle, sunburns appear,
While beach balls engage in a wild frontier.

The locals make jokes, they've got the flair,
As palm trees sway without a care.
Cocktails are clinking, laughter abounds,
Oh, what a joy this good vibe surrounds!

Colors of the Currents

The ocean is painting with hues so bright,
A dolphin in shades is quite a sight.
Fish dance like confetti in sparkly shows,
While a crab rolls by in a brand new pose.

Shells are the treasures in this funny dance,
Each wave brings laughter, and splashes of chance.
A sea urchin whispers, what's it all mean?
Surf's up, and come join, it's a colorful scene!

Stories from the Shoreline

A sandcastle stands, wonky and proud,
Fueled by giggles, a clap from the crowd.
Seashells share secrets, whispering low,
As starfish tell tales of the ebb and flow.

The sun begins setting, painting the sky,
With hues of laughter, oh my oh my!
A crab starts a party, it's quite the affair,
Join in the fun, leave your worries somewhere!

Serene Shores

On a beach where seagulls play,
I lost my flip-flop, what a day!
With sand between my toes, I grin,
But crabs think my foot's their kin.

The sun's a blazing disco ball,
I dance, I trip, then take a fall.
Umbrella drinks are full of cheer,
Except when I spill them—oh dear!

A Shell's Song

I found a shell, it spoke to me,
Said, "Here's the secret to the sea!"
But all it said was 'sandy toes'
And how to wiggle, strike a pose.

I tried to dance; a crab judged me,
With sideways glances, oh so free.
So I twisted, twirled, then I slipped,
And into the waves, I happily dipped!

Castaway Chronicles

I sailed away on a snack raft,
With chips and dip—oh, what a craft!
But seagulls swooped, they stole my feast,
Now, I'm just a hungry beast.

I've made a friend, a coconut,
We chat and laugh, though it won't strut.
We play cards, with shells for chips,
And dream of dancing at beachy trips.

Gentle Currents

The tide pulls in, then takes me out,
I splash and giggle, scream and shout.
Mermaids wave with silly grins,
As I try to show off my spins.

I built a castle, tall and grand,
But the waves thought it was just a band.
They crashed and laughed, my joy a mess,
Now I'm just left with soggy dress!

Dancing with Dunes

The sand was hot, the sun was bright,
I tripped and fell, what a silly sight!
But up I jumped, with a goofy grin,
And danced with dunes, let the fun begin!

Seagulls laughed as they swooped low,
Stealing fries from my picnic show.
I waved my arms and made a scene,
As sand took my shoes for a wild routine!

The wind joined in with its playful tune,
We laughed and twirled beneath the moon.
Rolling waves sang a beachy song,
Together we danced all night long!

With grains of sand in every crack,
I thought to myself, there's no looking back.
Funny moments and sandy cheer,
This goofy life, I hold so dear!

Ebb and Flow of Time

The clock ticks slow on sun-kissed days,
As crabs engage in silly plays.
They scurry left, then dash to the right,
Chasing waves in sheer delight!

A coconut falls, oh what a thud!
And my sun hat takes a beachside flood.
Laughing at how the tide rolls in,
Time's a prankster, wearing a grin!

The seashells gossip, oh yes they do,
"Did you hear about Bob? He got muddy too!"
Each wave that comes carries tales anew,
Of sunbathers slipping and swimsuits askew!

We raise a toast to sandy feet,
To funny moments, life can't be beat.
In this ebb and flow, we simply rhyme,
Forever young, in the arms of time!

Sun-Soaked Adventures

Flip-flops squeaked on hot concrete,
As I stumbled over some fresh-cut meat!
A barbecue spread took us for a ride,
Grilling and giggling, with friends by my side.

Waves rolled in like a slide of fun,
And I took a trip, oh what a run!
Fell on my back with a splat and a splash,
A sun-filled day gone in a flash!

Chasing crabs with a keen delight,
They danced away with a shifty flight.
Next came the seagulls, bold and spry,
Stealing my sandwich, oh me, oh my!

With sun-kissed skin and laughter abound,
Each moment cherished, joy profound.
Adventures unfold with every sunbeam,
In this funny little beachtime dream!

Acoustic Shores

The guitars strummed by the sandy shore,
As laughter echoed, we wanted more.
A ukulele broke, with a twang and a pop,
Turning our jam into a hilarious flop!

Someone brought chips, and salsa went flying,
While a crab joined in, it looked like it's trying!
We played our tunes, while seagulls crooned,
Our beachside band, oh how it bloomed!

Each strum a giggle, each note a sigh,
Our silly songs made the sun blush high.
We sang of life, love, and lost flip-flops,
With a rhythm so funny, it never stops!

As the sun dipped low, the giggles grew wide,
In this ocean of joy, we felt the tide.
To acoustic shores, we raise our toast,
For laughter and music, we love the most!

Tropical Whispers

In hammock swinging, drinks afloat,
A parrot squawks, a silly note.
Coconuts drop with a splat,
As crabs roam free wearing a hat.

Sun shines bright on my snack stand,
While tourists jive, not quite so planned.
A beach ball rolls, oh what a chase,
And the seagulls laugh at my red face.

Sun-Kissed Serenity

Flip-flops flapping, a dance so grand,
With sunscreen slick on every hand.
A piña colada spills on my toes,
And laughter erupts as the tide flows.

My towel's gone, swept out to sea,
While I chase an ice cream, oh, woe is me!
Fish swim by wearing the latest shades,
And the sun-tanned tourists strike cool charades.

Waves of Solitude

The waves come crashing with a giggle,
I try to surf, but I just wiggle.
Seashells whisper secrets sweet,
While crabs compete in a dance-off feat.

Beneath the sun, I take a nap,
Awoken by a beach ball's slap.
Jellyfish wearing tiny ties,
Float by just to catch my eyes.

Palm Shadows at Dusk

Palm trees sway like crazy dancers,
While I attempt my clumsy prancers.
A lizard struts, with style to spare,
While I trip over my own two air.

The sunset paints the sky with flair,
As snacks of guacamole fill the air.
A crab in shades steals my last fry,
And I chuckle loud, as the dolphins fly.

Breath of the Wind

A gust blew in on a lazy day,
It whisked my hat right away.
Chasing it down, I trip and fall,
Laughing out loud, I can't help but sprawl.

A seagull squawks, a fishy delight,
It steals my sandwich, takes to flight.
I wave my fists, but all in jest,
The sun's shining bright, I feel so blessed.

Paradise Found

Woke up to find my drink's gone missing,
The ice cubes clink, the waves are kissing.
Pineapples dance in my fruit salad bowl,
They giggle and sway, they play their role.

A crab plays tag, oh what a sight,
He scuttles away, oh, what a fright!
I laugh and dive into the sea foam,
In this funny place, I've found my home.

A Canvas of Blue

The sky's a canvas, a splash of cheer,
I paint with clouds that drift near.
My brush gets high when the wind does blow,
A rainbow splash—oh look at it glow!

A dolphin jumps, does a flip and twirl,
I clap my hands, give a laugh, and whirl.
Nature's the artist, I'm just the fan,
Creating magic with every plan.

Mermaid's Lullaby

The mermaid sings by the reef at night,
Her voice is sweet, her laugh's a delight.
Fish gather round, they wiggle and sway,
   While I giggle and cheer her way.

A sea turtle dreams of a dance so grand,
   With disco lights on the golden sand.
   I join in, making silly moves,
In this underwater groove, we all improve!

Beneath the Coconut Canopy

Coconuts drop with a thud,
As I sip on my coconut bud.
A crab scuttles, pinching my toe,
This island life sure steals the show.

Seagulls squawk, looking for snacks,
While I dodge waves and playful wacks.
Sunburnt and silly in flip flops,
My laughter echoes as my drink pops.

Palm trees sway with a gentle sway,
Though my hat flies off and drifts away.
I chase after it, rush like a fool,
The ocean's my dance floor, the sand's my pool.

Beneath this canopy, I'm not alone,
With friends who laugh, we're in our zone.
We make sand castles, some quite absurd,
With lopsided towers, laughter is stirred.

Laughter on the Shore

Waves crash, tickling my toes,
While a seagull steals fries from my nose.
I wave back, it's all in good fun,
Under the bright, blazing sun.

Beach balls bounce, we play toss and catch,
Someone's hat flies off—oh what a match!
We giggle and run, our spirits take flight,
Chasing the sunset, what a delight!

Sandy sandwiches, what a strange treat,
With sunburned faces, it can't be beat.
A sand dollar found, oh what a score,
We laugh till we drop, then we laugh some more.

As night falls, we dance on the shore,
With laughter and joy, who could ask for more?
Under the stars, our hearts feel so light,
This beachy gathering feels just right.

Dusk at the Dunes

The sun dips low, painting the sky,
As I flip in the sand, oh my, oh my!
With a belly flop, I land with a thud,
Laughing so hard, I roll in the mud.

Tide pools shimmer with shells and delights,
We race to find treasures, our playful sights.
A hermit crab scolds me, how rude indeed,
But I laugh it off, it's just what I need.

The breeze brings whispers, secrets so sweet,
While my friend gets stuck in a sandcastle seat.
We can't help but giggle, it's all part of fun,
At dusk by the dunes, where the wild things run.

Stars start to blink as we pack up the night,
With salty good vibes, oh what a sight!
Bonfire tales and silly-old songs,
In this sandy haven where laughter belongs.

A Journey to Calm

With flip-flops flapping, we venture afar,
Sending our worries to the nearest star.
A hammock waits, swinging like a dream,
While I sip on a drink, all is as it seems.

The breeze chuckles, whispering low,
As I nap in the shade where the palm trees grow.
A splash from the ocean brings me awake,
With a seagull nearby, eyeing my cake.

The surf rolls in, like a playful pup,
Who knew relaxing could be so much fun?
I plead with the tide to keep it at bay,
But it winks and retreats, no need to stay.

As the sun turns to gold, my heart beats in tune,
With a smile on my face like a bright silver moon.
Here in this paradise, everything's right,
A journey to calm, pure joy in the night.

Sunlit Pathways

In flip-flops on the sand, we play,
With sunburned noses come what may.
Hiding from crabs that scuttle and roam,
We chuckle as one tries to claim our home.

A seagull swoops, it steals our fries,
We laugh while chasing, oh what a surprise!
Sandy sandwiches, a picnic delight,
Yet somehow we've turned it into a fight!

With ice cream dripping down our hands,
We dance around as the music strands.
Coconut drinks with paper umbrellas,
Are perfect props for silly fellas.

As the sun sets with colors so bright,
We gather for stories, our hearts feeling light.
Each laugh a treasure, each moment we keep,
On this sunlit path, we share and leap.

The Call of Quicksand

We tiptoe near the mystery bog,
Laughing as we watch a lazy dog.
"Don't step there!" shouts a friend in fright,
But we wade in, fueled by sheer delight.

Stuck in the muck, we wiggle and squirm,
Trading our shoes for a newfound term.
"Fashionable" was not the plan,
But quicksand makes a funky tan!

The frogs all croak, they laugh in glee,
While we're trapped in muddy jubilee.
We take selfies, looking quite absurd,
In the goo—oh, how we're unheard!

Finally freed, we wave with pride,
Covered in muck, we stride with wide-eyed.
Who knew that fun could cause such a mess?
In the call of quicksand, we found our success!

Waterslide Whispers

A twisty slide with leaks and thrills,
We race down, laughter spills and chills.
Screams erupt, a watery dance,
As we fly down, caught in a chance.

Splash zone warnings were made for naught,
Drenched from head to toe, we bought the plot.
"I'll beat you!" shouts my brother with cheer,
But he zooms past, I can only sneer.

Rubber ducks bobbing to the beat,
We giggle, holding onto our seat.
With each twist, T-boned by a friend,
Who knew waterslides had such a blend?

At day's end, the pool is our stage,
Chatting and splashing, we act our age.
In these whispers of waves and sun,
Waterslide memories—oh what fun!

A Sailor's Pilgrimage

With a cardboard boat, we set out to sea,
The neighbors laugh, perhaps they're not free.
X marks the spot, so we chart our course,
But wind from the fridge? We're feeling remorse!

Plastic swords in hand, we shout with glee,
Imaginary pirates? Just you and me!
We threaten the waves with a jellybean snack,
"You'll walk the plank, if you dare attack!"

The sea's not so scary when we wear our caps,
Sailing through puddles, avoiding the traps.
"Ahoy there, mateys!" we laugh and we croon,
Our toilet-paper sails flapping 'neath the moon.

As the sun sets, we dock with a cheer,
The journey is silly, but oh-so dear.
With all of our dreams packed safely away,
A sailor's pilgrimage, joy rules the day!

Saltwater Serenade

The sun shines bright, our spirits soar,
We dance with seagulls and ask for more.
A splash of salt and a crispy fry,
Who needs a boat when you can just fly?

Flip-flops flop as we shimmy and sway,
Crabs join our fiesta, hip-hip hooray!
With coconuts filled, we sing out loud,
Even the fish think we're quite the crowd.

A wave crashes in, it joins the fun,
Surfboards in hand, we race the sun.
Laughter echoes, the sky's so clear,
As dolphins giggle, let's give a cheer!

So grab your shades and put on your hat,
Join our conga line, say, "Look at that!"
We'll build a sand castle, tall and grand,
And let the tide wash away our plans!

Breeze Through the Mangroves

In the shade where the wild things play,
We swap our worries for a fun-filled day.
The breeze is cheeky, plays with our hair,
It tickles our noses, life without care.

Skimming stones while the crabs do stroll,
Each splash is a laugh, that's our goal!
We taste the air, it's salty and sweet,
Hide and seek with iguanas on our feet.

At dusk when the sun paints the sky,
We throw a beach party and don't be shy.
Mangoes are flying, and laughter spreads,
Toasting the night with pancakes instead!

The stars come out, all twinkly and bright,
As we tell tall tales until the fall of night.
Let's dance like no one's watching our moves,
As the moon joins in on our groovy grooves!

The Color of Coral

Coral reefs sparkle in sunbeam's delight,
With colors buzzing like bees in flight.
A parrotfish prances, it's quite the sight,
Even the starfish join in the plight.

Fish in tuxedos swim past the clown,
They giggle at everyone, wearing a frown.
Anemones wave, saying, "Come join us!"
But we've lost our pants; oh, what a fuss!

The ocean's a stage, with seaweed ballet,
The krill do the cha-cha, then sprinkle all day.
Jellyfish float like balloons in a spree,
And here comes a turtle, "Hey, just let me be!"

So splash in the waves, let's dive and play,
In this watercolor dream where we laugh away.
With seashells in pockets and sand in our hair,
We'll call it a night with a giggling flair!

Sands of Solitude

Upon the soft sands, I flop like a fish,
Dreaming of snacks and the fanciest dish.
The waves whisper secrets, I hear them tell,
About sunny days and things that went well.

A crab scuttles by with a pop and a slide,
While I try to stand up, it fills me with pride!
I wobble and giggle, the sun's getting low,
Then trip on my towel, with a crash and a 'whoa!'

Seagulls squawk loudly, they steal my fries,
I barter with laughter, to win back my prize.
"Take my hat!" I shout, as they swoop on down,
Wearing my sunblock, I'll be the toast of the town!

The moon rises high, a disco ball bright,
We dance on the shoreline, all through the night.
With footprints in sand, and memories to save,
I'll giggle in solitude, happy and brave!

Nature's Embrace

In the sun, I lost my hat,
A seagull stole it, how about that?
Sand stuck in my ice cream cone,
Nature's jokes, I'm not alone!

The waves dance like they're in a race,
Splashing water, a funny face.
Crabs perform their sideways prance,
As if they're caught in a wild dance!

Coconuts drop with a thud,
I'm dodging them, oh what a dud!
Laughter echoes in the salty air,
Nature's embrace, I do declare!

With each chuckle, my worries fade,
In this paradise, I'm unafraid.
The sun sets with a golden wink,
Nature's humor makes me think!

Reflections in the Tide.

A mirror lake, oh what a sight,
Fish swim by, oh what a flight!
Reflections laugh with each soft wave,
Nature's jesters, oh how they pave!

Splashing kids, their giggles loud,
Making friends with clouds, so proud.
A beach ball flies, free as a kite,
Chasing shadows, a playful fight!

Sunbathers snooze under palm's shade,
Dreaming of adventures they made.
Upon the shore, where laughter hides,
Reflections dance with low tides.

Seashells whisper silly tales,
Of fishy friends and windy gales.
With each splash and each playful glide,
Life's a laugh at the ocean's side!

Tides of Serenity

Waves tickle toes on sandy shores,
A seagull squawks, it wants the scores.
Buckets and shovels lie beside,
Building castles, oh what a ride!

The sunset spills in a paintbox hue,
Kids giggle, slipping in their shoe.
Tides roll in with a cheeky grin,
Bringing treasures like a dance begin!

The ice cream truck is a sweet parade,
With every lick, my worries fade.
Funny tan lines are now a thing,
In a beach ball war, who will win?

In this place of sun-soaked bliss,
Life's jokes come wrapped in a salty kiss.
Nature holds us in her sway,
In waves that laugh and play all day!

Whispering Palms

Palms sway gently, sharing secrets here,
Whispers of breezes, oh so clear.
A crab in a shell thinks he's a knight,
Defending his turf with all his might!

Sunburned tourists, all in a mess,
Trying to relax, but I must confess.
Sandy snacks slowly drift away,
Dancing on breezes like it's their day!

Tiki torches flicker, shadows play,
While squawking parrots start their fray.
Laughter bubbles like soda that popped,
In this land where worries are dropped!

As night falls, stars start to peek,
I duck into laughter, no time to speak.
With every giggle, a memory blooms,
In this paradise, all fun resumes!

Feathered Friends of the Coast

Seagulls squawking, what a show,
Diving for fries, they steal the dough.
With flapping wings and sassy styles,
They strut around with goofy smiles.

Crows in sunglasses, looking fly,
Stealing snacks as people cry.
Chickens dance in the morning light,
Pecking at crumbs, oh what a sight!

Pelicans fish with grace and flair,
Belly flops land them in mid-air.
Waddling ducks in hats parade,
Making waves in the sun and shade.

All the ruckus, all the cheer,
Feathered friends bring fun this year.
With laughter echoing by the sea,
Who knew birds could be such glee?

Windswept Memories

The breeze is ticklish, what a thrill,
Twirling hats, oh won't they spill!
Kites are dancing, up they soar,
Lost my sandwich—now who wants more?

Sunburnt noses, laughter loud,
Umbrellas flip, oh what a crowd!
Chasing crabs down the sandy lane,
Dancing in circles, feeling no pain.

Windswept hair and salty cheeks,
Giggling at all the funny freaks.
Ice cream drips, a sticky race,
Chasing memories at a silly pace.

Every gust, a joyful scream,
Windy days are a dreamer's dream.
In the chaos, we can all see,
Life's a laugh by the wild, blue sea.

Luminescent Shores

Moonlit waters, shimmering bright,
Glow-in-the-dark crabs take flight.
Fireflies join in the ocean's light,
They dance and flicker, what a sight!

Bioluminescence, nature's art,
Splash a wave, create a spark.
Frogs in sunglasses sing a tune,
Underneath the smiling moon.

Glow sticks bobbing, a party on sand,
Here's to fun, let's make a stand.
Turtles grooving, crabs with flair,
Every creature aware, full of care.

Late-night giggles, what a blast,
Memories made forever last.
In the twinkles, we find our score,
Dancing together on luminescent shores.

Footprints in the Soft Sand

Jogging on grains, oh what a mess,
Footprints crisscross, we all confess.
Slippery shells, I trip and fall,
But laughter echoes; I still stand tall.

Kids building castles, what a scene,
With moats of water, oh so keen.
Sandy snacks make sticky hands,
While gulls plot schemes, making demands.

Jumping over waves, the tide retreats,
Wet socks are funny, yet life's sweet treats.
Chasing sunsets, oh what a race,
Finding footprints, leaving no trace.

Every step tells a tale anew,
In soft, warm sand, we laugh and grew.
So let's make tracks, it's time to play,
With footprints in the sun each day.

Barefoot Dreams

Sun-kissed toes in squishy sand,
Crabs scuttle by, oh isn't it grand?
Flip-flops left, let the laughter flow,
Dance like nobody, just go with the show.

Seashells whisper secrets to the shore,
A seagull steals fries, oh what a chore!
Roll in the surf, make a splashy route,
Laughter bubbles when we fall and shout.

Coral Breezes

Waves tickle feet, a salty spray,
A coconut surprise, who took it away?
Silly hats and shades, misplaced on the floor,
Laughter echoes as we find them once more.

Fish in bright colors gaze with a grin,
While we attempt to dive, but just spin!
Giggling mermaids, in our dreams they tease,
Stealing our hearts with oceanic ease.

The Rhythm of the Tides

Every wave's a joke, swirling with glee,
Belly flops and giggles, oh what a spree!
Sandy sandwiches and clumsy sunburns,
Nature's charm gives plenty of turns.

Dancing shells under the glowing light,
Crabby conquests take a frantic flight!
Visit the tide pools, peek and explore,
Finding lost treasures, we always want more.

Paradise Found

A hammock sways, bugs flying around,
Who invited them? Not us, that's how it's found!
We toast with pineapples, laughter the drink,
In this paradise, we barely can think.

Kites that tumble, winds that won't care,
Tangled in laughter, we float in the air.
Moments like these, we gladly embrace,
With sunburned noses, we run this wild race.

Cerulean Echoes

Beneath a sun with a laughing face,
Where flip-flops race in a sand-filled space,
Seagulls chatter like gossiping friends,
While surfboards dance, the fun neverends.

A crab in a hat takes a stroll at noon,
Sipping coconut juice with a big silver spoon,
A starfish whispers its oceanic glee,
"Come join the party, just you and me!"

The waves throw jokes that splash with a grin,
While fish wear sunglasses as they dive in,
A buoy waves hello, it's quite the surprise,
With a wink as if to say, "Don't be shy!"

So laugh with the tides, let your worries cease,
Where the sand tickles toes and laughter's the lease,
In this cerulean world, play a silly tune,
As the palm trees sway to the afternoon moon.

Untold Myths of the Ocean

Beneath the waves where tales are spun,
A mermaid sings in a voice so fun,
"Forget the sailors, take a break from strife,
Come join my dance, it's a splash of life!"

A dolphin dives with a flip of flair,
While octopuses juggle without a care,
Their laughter bubbles in the salty spray,
Creating mischief in a whimsical way.

A treasure chest spills its glittering gold,
But it's just chocolate, or so I'm told,
A pirate parrot squawks, "Join the feast!"
With sweets in the sea, we're never least!

So dive into legends, those funny oddities,
With sea life sharing their jolly comedies,
In the depths of the blue, let smiles arise,
Where untold myths bring the biggest highs.

Rhythms of Remote Bays

In a cove where the sun plays peek-a-boo,
The tide hums along, as if it knew,
A crab plays the drums on a coconut shell,
While jellyfish twirl in a rhythmic swell.

Palm trees sway in sync with the beat,
With coconuts clapping their makeshift feet,
A group of fish throws a disco party,
Glittering scales making it quite hearty.

The waves whisper tales of the days gone past,
Of sunken ships and sea kings steadfast,
But they joke about mermaids who try to fly,
"Darling, stay grounded, and just wave hi!"

So unravel the rhythms, tap your toes in sand,
Join the chorus of sea life, oh isn't it grand?
For in these remote bays, we find delight,
With nature's laughter echoing day and night.

Nautical Daydreams

A parrot perched high with a pirate's grin,
Claims to know where the treasure's been,
With a map that's just ketchup spilled on a plate,
"Follow me, matey, we'll seal your fate!"

A sailboat drifts with a heart made of cheese,
Sailing through clouds, it does as it please,
While a wave looks up with an oceanic cheer,
"Hey crew, grab a snack, let's make this clear!"

Seagulls play bingo with shiny old spoons,
And fish throw a bash under bright, playful moons,
Where every splash is a chorus in tune,
Sailing through dreams, we'll party till June.

So set your sails to the winds of your dreams,
Where laughter is gold and fun is the theme,
In nautical tales spun from sun and sea,
Let your heart navigate, it's wild and free!

The Cove's Caress

In the cove where seagulls dance,
The crabs pinch hard, they take a chance.
A beach ball floats, it's not quite round,
While sunscreen's smeared, we all fall down.

Palm trees sway, they wiggle and sway,
A coconut lands, we're all in dismay.
With laughter bubbling, like soda pop,
Watch out, my friend, don't let your flip-flop drop.

Under sunrays, every laugh's a blast,
A fish stole my snack; it swam away fast.
All the sandcastles lean to one side,
But we just smile, in the fun we abide.

As day turns to night, we gather for fun,
And toast to mischief with a coconut bun.
Under the stars, our giggles arise,
In this wacky place, under merry skies.

Beneath a Sapphire Sky

Beneath the blue where the mermaids sing,
A dolphin pranks, and the seaweed clings.
With ice cream melting onto our toes,
A pelican swoops, where it landed? Who knows!

The boogie board's wearing a goofy grin,
As we try to surf with no chance to win.
Flip-flops flying with every wild crash,
The waves giggle too, in a frothy splash.

Caught in the sea, we're all one big mess,
Sunburned noses, but we couldn't care less.
Our lemonade's fizzy, the limes jump around,
Life's a party where joy can be found.

As evening approaches with a wobbly zap,
We'll roast marshmallows and take a quick nap.
Under stars that twinkle, we'll dance round and round,
In this silly place where our hearts are unbound.

Roaming the Reef

Roaming the reef, with goggles on tight,
A clownfish waves, say hello, what a sight!
With bubble-blowing contests all day long,
Even the octopus hums a quick song.

A sea turtle winks, oh, that's kind of cute,
While jellyfish drift in a wobbly suit.
"Why did the coral cross the shore?"
To find some new friends, that's for sure!

With treasure maps leading us to a snack,
A hidden cache of crispy fish flack.
The sea star grins, it's wide as can be,
In this weird world, everyone's silly and free.

As the sun dips down with a splash of pink,
We cherish these moments, take a quick wink.
A chorus of laughter fills up the air,
In this funny old place, with no worries or care.

Saltwater Awakening

In the morning sun, the beach awakens,
With a taco truck, we're feeling unshaken.
The surf's rolling in, but so is a wave,
Of jokester seagulls, what silliness they'll pave.

Strutting about in our best summer gear,
With mismatched swimsuits, there's nothing to fear.
A sand dollar laughs, rolling in with the tide,
We'll gather our treasures with glee as our guide.

Our morning yoga becomes a big flop,
A crab creeps in and makes us all stop.
"Are you ready for downward dog?" one yells,
The crabs applaud; they know all the swells.

As sun sets low, with a wink and a cheer,
We toast to the mishaps, with friends always near.
In this quirky haven, filled with delight,
We laugh and we play, under soft firelight.

Moments on the Coast

Seagulls squawk, what a sight,
Chasing chips, they take flight.
A crab walks sideways with such grace,
Seems he's winning the food race.

Sandy toes and salty hair,
Kids scream loud without a care.
A beach ball bounces, and oh dear,
It smacks a sunbather—laughter near!

Sunburns forming, red and bright,
Lotion battles, what a fight!
Pineapple drinks with little straws,
Cheers to fun, and no real cause!

When the tide pulls back its might,
Shells are treasures, oh what a sight!
But watch your step, oh don't you trip,
That conch shell's got a wicked grip!

Horizon's Call

The sun dips low, a golden ball,
We pretend to surf, but we all fall.
Flip-flops flying, laughter erupts,
Matching swimsuits? Nope! That's corrupt!

Friends with drinks, they strike a pose,
Tropical hats with silly bows.
A stray dog joins, thinks he's part,
He lounges close, capturing hearts.

Seashells traded for sunburned backs,
We skewer snacks with tiny tacks.
A game of beach-tag, what a thrill,
Tripping on sandbags, now that's skill!

The twilight whispers, stars appear,
With dreams of food and ice-cold beer.
The breeze tells tales, oh so funny,
With friends around, life is sunny!

An Evening in the Tropics

The tiki torches dance at night,
We sip our drinks, all feels right.
A parrot squawks, "Tell me a joke!"
We share one so bad, almost choke!

Footloose friends on a sandy floor,
Hula dancing, what a score!
Someone trips, the music squeaks,
Laughter erupts; we're all on fleek!

The night's alive with giggles bright,
We roast marshmallows, what a sight!
A firework screams, pops up high,
"Oops!" we say, as it flies by!

At last, the stars put on their show,
We pine for snacks, but who could know?
The pizza man arrives on time,
Somehow a pineapple made it prime!

Lanterns on the Water

Lanterns float with gentle grace,
Reflecting smiles on each face.
The frogs croak tunes, a perfect band,
Grab the snacks—hush hush, don't get banned!

A rubber duck floats, what a sight,
The dog's convinced it's a fight.
A splash here, a splash there, what fun it seems,
We're living life, chasing silly dreams!

Glow sticks shine in vivid hues,
A dance-off starts; who'll win? We choose!
Everyone's twirling in a silly way,
As lanterns giggle, they join the play.

With waves that lap and giggles near,
We raise a toast and share the cheer.
The moon above laughs with delight,
As we create our own starry night!

Sunsets and Sea Glass

The sun waves goodbye, wearing orange and pink,
Seagulls are gossiping, what do they think?
Flip-flops are squeaking, the sand's a delight,
While crabs have a dance-off, what a silly sight!

Tanned toes in the water, making quite the splash,
A flip-flop's betrayal, oh, what a clash!
Laughter erupts, as drinks spill on the mat,
Life's glass half-full, until the seabird sat!

Sandcastles tumble, under waves they collapse,
With shells as our jewels, we're all in mishaps.
The sunset's a painter, wild and absurd,
As we collect sea glass, not a single word!

Yet the night brings a glow, with fireflies in flight,
S'mores are the highlight, oh what a delight!
Happiness lingers, like the scent of sea salt,
Turning moments to memories, that's our real vault!

Echoes of the Shore

The waves come crashing, with a giggle and roar,
Shells whisper secrets, from the depths of the shore.
Seagulls on duty, they'll steal your fries,
While we chase the sunset, beneath candy skies!

Kites in the sky, like they're having a race,
While toddlers are making, a very strange face!
A surfboard's a throne, for a crab and a sock,
Two lizards are bickering, on a sun-warmed rock!

Ice cream is melting, on a hot summer's day,
Sweet drips down our hands, in a funny display.
Mermaids are laughing, while we splash and play,
Echoes of giggles, in the warmth of the bay!

As twilight approaches, the stars start to peek,
Our beach towels fold up, with stories to speak.
We'll dream of tomorrow, with laughter and cheer,
More echoes of joy, on the shores we hold dear!

Driftwood Memories

A piece of driftwood, as crooked as me,
A throne for the crabs, by the sparkling sea.
Old flip-flops lay scattered, like shoes gone astray,
And laughter rings out, in a pirate's ballet!

The sun's doing squats, as it inches down low,
While beach bums doze off, in rows like a show.
Seagulls are plotting, to steal all the fries,
As treasure maps hand-drawn, become silly lies!

A sandbar emerged, like a dance floor at dusk,
With conga lines formed, though no one can trust.
Tacos in hand, we toast with our shells,
To driftwood adventures, and sweet tales we tell!

The tide rolls back, drawing memories in,
Every grain of sand, holds a giggle within.
We gather our treasures, with joy and delight,
And vow to return, under soft moonlit night!

A Breeze Between Palms

Palm trees are swaying, with a rhythm so spry,
They shake their green heads, as the seagulls fly by.
We dance with the breeze, under skies oh-so-blue,
While sunscreen's a battle, we're trying to skew!

Flip-flops perplexed, in a game of their own,
One flies in the air, and the other just moans.
Beach games are absurd, who made up that rule?
As we throw water balloons, like we're still in school!

The sun is a baker, whipping up golden,
With laughter and sprinkles, our joy is beholden.
A crab's in a hurry, scuttling right past,
While the shadows grow long, oh, how summer's fast!

As evening arrives, we gather with glee,
Around a bonfire, sharing tales by the sea.
The breeze brings us whispers, of fun times long gone,
And we smile at each other, as we bask till the dawn!

Sun-Kissed Dreams

Under the sun, we dance and play,
Sipping cool drinks, melting the day.
Flip-flops squeak on the sandy floor,
Crabs doing the cha-cha, oh what a score!

Seashells whisper secrets to the shore,
While seagulls squawk, begging for more.
Laughter bounces like balls thrown high,
As we all pretend to be a butterfly!

Sunsets paint skies in orange and pink,
With snacks of coconut, we joyfully wink.
The sky's a canvas for our quirky arts,
As we forget our worries and silly parts!

Even the fish seem to wear a grin,
Waving their fins, they invite us in.
In our sun-kissed dreams, life's a big show,
Where humor dances, and good vibes flow!

Echoes of the Ocean

The waves clap back with a cheeky cheer,
Crashing like toddlers, loud and near.
Sea turtles bob, wearing hats of foam,
They wave their flippers, welcome us home!

Barnacles gossip on rocks with glee,
Shells rolling by, they're laughing at me.
Dolphins dive in, with flips in the spray,
Showing off shows in a splashy ballet!

Mermaids giggle, hiding from sight,
Painting their tails with shells, oh what a sight!
The sun's golden rays, a twist of lime,
Makes every moment feel just divine!

Catch a seagull, they steal your fries,
Chasing them down, what a funny surprise!
With the ocean's echoes, let's jump and sing,
In this whimsical world, we're the ocean's bling!

Tropical Tranquility

In hammocks swaying, we drift and sway,
Telling tall tales that chase clouds away.
Pineapples frown at the sun's bright might,
And coconuts giggle, oh what a sight!

Palms dance gently, waving hello,
While parrots squawk how they steal the show.
The breeze hums a tune, a soft serenade,
As we sip our drinks under palm tree shade.

Kids chase each other, quite the parade,
Stumbling and giggling, oh how they've played!
With sand in our toes, we can't help but grin,
In this chilling haven, let the fun begin!

The sun sets slowly, a fluorescent ball,
We dance like nobody, no cares at all.
In tropical peace, let the laughter reel,
For in this paradise, joy's what we feel!

The Rhythm of Waves

The waves have a beat, a bubbly sound,
Bouncing along, round and round.
Crashing and splashing, a silly dance,
Sandcastles crumbling, you stand no chance!

Seashells beatbox with every swell,
Whispers of the ocean, a funny spell.
Fishes swim by in disco attire,
Jiving to rhythms that never tire!

The sun, a drummer, keeps the pace,
While crabs join in with their sideways grace.
With a flip of a tail, and a wink of an eye,
The ocean's a stage, under the sky!

As twilight creeps in, the stars appear,
Campfire stories ignite the cheer.
With every laughter, a wave we embrace,
In this funky concert, we've found our place!

Harmony in the Haze

In shades of green, we sway and toast,
Laughter rings out, a joyful boast.
The breeze plays tricks with our hair so wild,
As we dance like a carefree child.

Umbrellas tilt in a clumsy fight,
Sunscreen battles in the midday light.
We slip on flip-flops, a comedic trudge,
While seagulls laugh, in a feathery judge.

Coconuts laugh from their lofty throne,
As we spill drinks, and all that we've known.
The rhythm of waves, a wobbly beat,
We stumble and tumble on warm, sandy feet.

So here we gather, a mismatched crew,
Trading silly stories, all fresh and new.
In this haze of fun, we lose track of time,
A perfect mix of the foolish and sublime.

Sanctuary of the Sea

The tides are high, the snacks are too,
I brought the chips; did you bring the brew?
Waves crash and giggle, a frothy laugh,
As we plot our next sun-soaked photograph.

My hat's a sail, it's caught in the breeze,
You chase my napkin—oh, if you please!
Laughter erupts as it flies like a kite,
We yell and we cheer, what a comical sight!

The sun starts to sink, painting the sky,
We pretend to swim, but really we lie.
With toes in the sand, we build a grand fort,
A masterpiece built from each silly report.

As darkness creeps in, we roast marshmallows,
Telling wild tales that make us all howls.
In this sanctuary where laughter resounds,
The sea whispers stories; its humor abounds.

Floating Dreams

On pink floaties, we drift with delight,
Bobbing and bouncing, what a silly sight!
We splash like dolphins in awkward arcs,
While the sun paints our skin with soft sparks.

A snack raft appears, with goodies galore,
We munch on chips, while craving some more.
Sips of bright drinks send us into a spin,
As our grandpa's jokes start to wear thin.

The clouds flirt over, like marshmallows high,
We wave at each one, as it drifts by.
The floaties giggle, they twist and they twirl,
Caught in the chaos of a splashy whirl.

As twilight approaches, we still float around,
Making up songs, the silliest found.
In this dreamy state, all worries dissolve,
With laughter and joy, we hum and revolve.

Tale of Two Tides

With one tide to the left, and one to the right,
We stroll down the beach, in pure delight.
You trip on a shell, and I burst in glee,
Is this a dance? A slip? Just you and me!

The sun is a clown, in orange and pink,
Waving hello with a wink and a blink.
At the water's edge, we write in the sand,
With doodles and dreams all carefully planned.

Seashells collect our tales of the day,
Each one a giggle in the salt-sprayed play.
We trade funny faces, and playful jibes,
Mischief abounds in our sandy vibes.

As the final wave curls and takes its cue,
We laugh as we scramble, like kids in a zoo.
In this tale of two tides, oh what a spree,
Heartfelt laughter flows wild and free.

Lost in Lullabies

Swaying palm trees whisper jokes,
Sandy crabs wearing tiny cloaks.
Sleepy waves hum goofy tunes,
While seagulls dance beneath the moons.

Tropical breezes tickle my nose,
A friendly parrot strikes silly poses.
Under stars, my laughter blooms,
Floating dreams in colorful plumes.

Flip-flops squeak with each big step,
I trip on shells, but here's the prep:
A cocktail spills, a splash, a shout,
In paradise, we laugh it out.

So here I lay, the world amiss,
Counting giggles, not a thing to miss.
The waves keep rolling, jokes on repeat,
Lost in lullabies, life's goofy beat.

Coral Gardens

Beneath the sea, fish wear their hats,
Coral blooms like funky mats.
Starfish partying, quite a sight,
Tickling turtles join in the night.

A clownfish tells a witty tale,
While jellyfish float like a sail.
They've got moves that make me snort,
In this underwater, silly court.

Sea cucumbers, they simply chill,
Dropping puns, testing their skill.
Anenomes wave, waving hello,
In coral gardens, laughter flows.

Bubbles rise like giggles free,
Underwater chuckles, can't you see?
Life in the ocean, with a twist,
Washed away worries, nothing missed.

Glistening Tributes

Sunshine glimmers, a disco ball,
Waves crash down, like nature's call.
Seashells gathering for a toast,
Salty sea air, we laugh the most.

The sun takes selfies with the beach,
Caught in a wave, it's out of reach!
Seagulls squawking their daily news,
While flip-flops shuffle, sharing views.

Ocean breeze spreads giggles wide,
Coconuts laughing on this ride.
Each splash a tribute to the fun,
Under a sky that's brightly spun.

Dance with crabs in the golden light,
Every moment feels so right.
Glistening tributes, we're all part,
Laughter and joy, a life's fine art.

Shores of Reflection

Waves whisper secrets, so absurd,
Each splash carries a funny word.
Footprints dancing on warm sand,
Echoes of laughter, oh so grand.

Flip-flops flip in a comic parade,
Seagulls swoop in mischief displayed.
The sun waves back with playful rays,
Chasing shadows in joyful plays.

Turtles plod with a purposeful strut,
While crabs giggle, caught in a rut.
Sunsets paint skies with goofy flair,
In the twilight, we find our share.

Shores of reflection, we take a bow,
Collecting chuckles, here and now.
In this moment, we feel alive,
With every wave, our spirits thrive.

Whims of the Wind

The breeze tickles my nose, oh what a prank,
Palm trees sway and giggle, down by the bank.
A crab in a tuxedo scuttles with flair,
While flip-flops complain of their sandy affair.

Seashells whisper secrets, or so they claim,
Each wave brings a joke, in its bubbly fame.
A seagull dives for lunch, but misses his aim,
And I laugh as he fluffs, feeling quite the same.

Sunburnt tourists tripping over their toes,
Chasing a rogue frisbee that nobody knows.
We dance on hot sand, in our sunhats galore,
While locals just chuckle, we're backs to the shore.

With piña coladas that taste like a dream,
We toast to good fortune, or so it would seem.
As laughter erupts like a fizzled-out spark,
We embrace every whim, till the sun starts to arc.

Crescent Moon Reflections

The moon hangs like a smile, up in the night,
Reflections of mermaids, oh what a sight!
A dolphin named Dave sings croons to the tide,
And we join in the chorus, with giggles wide.

Starfish wearing glasses, looking so wise,
Recounting tall tales underneath the bright skies.
While waves dance around us, swirling in cheer,
Each splash tells a joke, for all of us here.

A coconut falls and rolls down the sand,
Tickling our feet, oh isn't it grand?
We chase after laughs, like the breeze in our hair,
While crickets provide music, in cool evening air.

With sparklers and laughter, our candles aglow,
We sing to the moon, making memories flow.
As the night stretches on, in its shimmering cloak,
We find funny fortune in each little joke.

Festivities of the Faraway

A parade of bright colors, oh what a show,
Tropical tunes make everyone glow.
Hula skirts twirling, with laughter and cheer,
As a pineapple juggler draws all of us near.

The conch shells call out, signaling fun,
While locals dance wildly, soaking up sun.
A goat on a surfboard, yes, that's a sight,
As we all crack up during this festive night.

Taco trucks breeze by, wafting great smells,
With guacamole jokes, we're under its spells.
Every plate brings a grin, bursting with glee,
As snacks thrown like confetti cover you and me.

With glow sticks in hand, we frighten the dark,
As fireflies join in, with each little spark.
We laugh till we drop, under starlit display,
In festivities grand, we'll dance till the day.

Awakening the Aqua

Water flows gently, like a soft serenade,
Mermaids are morning, with coffee displayed.
A floatie named Freddy, bright pink and alive,
Tells jokes about dolphins, making waves thrive.

Sunlight giggles, reflecting on waves,
As fish pass in outfits, so funny it saves.
A snorkel fish grins, with a wink and a wave,
While we splash and we laugh, under ocean's knave.

A turtle in sunglasses, so sly and so chill,
Competes with a crab, at the top of the hill.
Winners get seaweed, draped over their heads,
While all join in laughter, "Who's counting?" it spreads.

We float through our day, in this aqua delight,
With playful connections making hearts feel light.
As sunset brings colors, so vibrant and rich,
We embrace all the quirks, and our spirits they lift.

www.ingramcontent.com/pod-product-compliance
Lightning Source LLC
Chambersburg PA
CBHW072129070526
44585CB00016B/1589